REMNANTS OF RESIDUE

FACING THE HIDDEN PAIN FROM THE PAST

SONIA MAYO

WESTBOW
PRESS®
A DIVISION OF THOMAS NELSON
& ZONDERVAN

WestBow Press books may be ordered through booksellers or by contacting:

WestBow Press
A Division of Thomas Nelson & Zondervan
1663 Liberty Drive
Bloomington, IN 47403
www.westbowpress.com
844-714-3454

ISBN: 978-1-6642-7176-0 (sc)
ISBN: 978-1-6642-7177-7 (e)

Library of Congress Control Number: 2022912536

Print information available on the last page.

WestBow Press rev. date: 11/4/2022

Contents

Acknowledgements

First, I'd like to thank God for giving me this message about Residue. It is a message that has been in my heart for a while now. It's the second time I've had the opportunity to write a book about residue because I felt that God said there was still more to share.

I'd like to thank my husband, Calvin Mayo for his support in pushing me and the constant reminders to finish the book.

Rebecca Francis, Beulah Martin, Elder Shontel Diggs and Shudine Covel, for taking the time to review the book, edit and give feedback several times as needed.

A special thanks also to these special women of Faith, who also held me accountable on many occasions, my mother Lillie White, Karen Bynum, Prophetess Trudey Crawford, Yanick Kane and Dr. Kim Johnson for their help, prayers and words of encouragement as well as so many other friends and family that supported and listened when I did not know what to do or how to finish this, I appreciate and love you all.

Introduction

Sometimes in life, we can be at the right place at the right time or the wrong place at the wrong time. Well, over 20 years ago, I was out with a friend of mine just having fun. We decided to go to this party on a military base. Well, that night, I had a little too much to drink and it caused me to be intoxicated to the point that I did not have any control over myself, and it drew the attention of two men. These men took advantage of the situation I was in and raped me. I was so intoxicated, that I did not even realize what was going on or what had happened to me until the next day.

So, time went by and the memory of what happened to me during that time never resurfaced, so I thought. You see, things can happen to you, and you don't know how they affect you. Tragedy can affect people in many ways without them even realizing it. I did not realize what had happened to me until God brought it to my attention twenty years later when I was asked to speak at a conference.

Why this incident was erased or blocked from my mind for so many years, I don't know. Some people can have a major tragedy happen and it can destroy them mentally, emotionally, or so many other ways because they just can't handle the idea or even the tormenting thought of what happened. Situations like this and so many others can leave residue and until it is confronted, and you are healed from it, it still has control over you in one way or another.

1

WHAT IS THIS RESIDUE?

R esidue is like a very strong root. You know roots like those of many huge old trees we see outside. They are hard to pull up by our bare hands or even a few simple tools. Just like most plants, the roots are hidden underground. They are not always readily visible. Sometimes you don't even know that they are there.

Roots

Roots that have been embedded in the ground for years and years take some very heavy-duty equipment to be removed, and if they grow under your walkway, driveway, or even your home, they can damage things unless they are properly removed and destroyed.

Years ago, at this townhouse I lived in, I had an issue with part of my walkway rising. I could not figure out why one step was higher than the other. I did not have the understanding or knowledge about cement. I just figured the previous owner messed it up some kind of way because the cement color on one part was lighter than the others. Well, I finally had it checked out and found out that the reason why part of my walkway was higher than another was because of the root from a tree that was previously there. This was odd to me because the tree wasn't there anymore. The tree was removed before I had ever moved in, but the root was not completely removed. It left something behind. Just like in our own lives, we can't see everything that's going on. Some things in our lives become hidden or suppressed and we become stuck. But when we open our hearts to God and allow him to come in, he opens our eyes to see things differently and clearer.

There are so many things that we encounter in life that can leave residue. Here are just a few:

Abandonment and Rejection (Rejected)

Merriam-Webster defines the following words:

Abandonment is the act of abandoning something or someone.

Over the years, my parents have had several foster children. Many children have been in the foster care system for years, moving from place to place, never really finding a permanent home. Some have struggled with running away, anger, and different types of addictions because of a parent, or someone really close to them, leaving them. They may have experienced rejection and disappointments as well.

When a person is rejected, they don't feel accepted. That can really destroy a person mentally and emotionally to the point that they may feel their life has no meaning or purpose, which can lead to being disappointed.

Rejected means not given approval or acceptance.

Disappointment the act or an instance of disappointing; the state or emotion of being disappointed.

Though some of these areas can start early on in life in childhood, they can affect a person well into adulthood if never addressed.

Unless we are willing to confront and destroy those things from our past, they will keep coming back up and affect our lives in one way or another. Some people say, "Yeah that person knew the right button to push," or "That person made me act that way". However, sometimes it was not the other person, but rather a reaction or response to what's already embedded in a person that they never confronted or destroyed.

Residue can form from so many life experiences that can leave leftover hurt or even pain from the past. It is not limited. It can affect the richest or poorest person in the world. This issue of residue is not just local, but international, meaning all over the world. It can affect anyone, anywhere, from all social classes.

From childhood, a person can be abused physically, emotionally, or even psychologically and feel they have no worth because that is what they were told. So that person grows up making poor decisions, unable to communicate effectively with others, or never excelling in life because they were told they couldn't.

In relationships, a person can be in a controlling relationship and feel that they can't make choices or have no say in anything and eventually they shut down. So, they avoid speaking up in life for fear that they will be attacked or told that no one wants to hear what they have to say. They become timid or passive, allowing others to take advantage of them or just walk all other them.

So many people deal with unresolved issues from the past that leave residue, and if they refuse to deal with it, it can lead to all types of addictions, habits, or even suicide.

My husband made a great point one day. He said residue is like a scar, always there. You can see it, it's a reminder that you have been hurt. With scars, we try to hide them and cover them up so that no one can see them. We don't want them to ask us what happened. We'd rather leave the scar, just like the pain, covered up so that we don't have to deal with it.

I began to explore the idea of residue in my own life when I was asked to speak at a conference. There were four of us speaking, and the subject that I was given to speak on was "How can you forgive when you can't forget?" I remember thinking, I don't have any unforgiveness against anyone that I can think of, so how can I speak on that?

Well, I looked up some scriptures on forgiveness and remember finding the story on the parable of the unforgiving debtor in Matthew 18:21-22, so I used that as part of the reasons we are to forgive and how we can achieve it. Beforehand, a friend of mine told me God was going to have me share something at the conference that I had forgotten about or had not shared with anyone. I don't remember exactly what she said, but that was the basis of it. So, the day finally came when I had to speak. I was so nervous and didn't know if I was going to be able to speak. I remember calling another friend who prayed for me because I had never been that nervous before. Maybe because this was an unknown crowd, I don't know. It took a while for me to calm down. When it was my turn, I just began to share about forgiveness, what the scripture said, and the importance of how God wants us to forgive not only others but ourselves.

That's when it happened–my message got interrupted with the story. All I could say was, wow, I didn't know I was going to share this. Now, all of a sudden, twenty years later, I was reminded of the pain I had endured from my past and it was time to share it.

My Story

This is the story I shared unexpectedly on the day I spoke on forgiveness. Early in my twenties, I was spending time together with a friend. We went to a party on a military base and had a great time, dancing, drinking, and socializing with the people there. Well, like most of us at times when we start drinking, we forget our limit because were having so much fun. By the time we start with one drink, here comes another and another, and before we know it, we drank way too much! Well, that's exactly what happened, I had too much to drink and was taken advantage of at the party. This is the reality of what can happen to a person when they don't have self-control. It allows others to take advantage of them. Now, I am not saying what they did was my fault. They were very wrong, and if I were in my right mind and not drunk, I could have filed charges against them both, but I was so confused at the time because I was so drunk and didn't realize the seriousness of what was happening to me.

Yes, it was rape. I was Violated! They took something that did not belong to them. They were trespassing. I think I was ashamed of saying that word for years, but it happened, at a party on a military base. However, it never affected me that I knew of because I just went on with my life and never gave it a second thought. I think part of me just reasoned, I was out at a party, drinking way too much, and that was the result of it. I didn't tell anyone other than my friend at that time, and we must have brushed it off I guess because I don't recall ever really talking about it again. We forgot about it, but God didn't.

So, as I was sharing that story at the conference, I felt like something was coming off me. I told them it was a spot God saw on me, and He wanted it off me, it was *residue*! Oh my! All these years it was on me, and I didn't even know it. It was hidden. But when you draw closer to God, to the light, things that were once hidden are exposed. They cannot hide anymore because God wants us healed and whole in him. He wants us Free!

If I was to go back and rehearse what took place before this conference, I recall attending at least three women's conferences where, in the end, they would ask if anyone wanted prayer for specific things. Most of the time they'd ask if anyone needed prayer in general, and sometimes they would specifically mention areas of healing, whether mental, emotional, or even physical. I was there, but each time I heard the offer for prayer, it never registered to me that I was a victim of any of those things, until one day. I attended a conference one day and my mom's friend happened to be there. She asked me a question after the conference. She was hesitant, but she proceeded to ask me anyway. She said, "Sonia, has anything like that ever happened to you"?

You see, at this conference, they were specific with the prayer requests. They mentioned physical abuse amongst other things. So, when she asked me, I just stood there, almost frozen. I replied, "Huh? Part of me was thinking, No, not me. Why would you ask me this? That question doesn't make sense.

You see, no one ever asked me about my past, and honestly, I had forgotten about it until that moment when it registered. After going through all these thoughts in my mind and trying to downplay everything as if that couldn't relate to me, the reality of it was that it did happen to me. It was shocking. Wow. God had been chasing me, trying to heal me, but I had dismissed it and didn't even acknowledge it as a problem or issue in my life until then. At that point, I knew God would not let this thing go, and he obviously wanted to do something about it. He wanted to remove the spot he saw, that spot was *residue!*

2

Exposing What's Hidden

W e must expose what's been hidden to be healed and totally free from the pain of the past. When you expose something, the dictionary says "you make (something) visible by uncovering it". WOW!!

My exposure came about at the conference. It was never supposed to be part of the message I was sharing that day, so I thought. But as I begin to speak about "How to forgive, when you can't forget," I immediately stopped. It was as if God said, ok now…and I remember saying, wow! I can't believe I'm about to share this. If you recall, earlier, God had sent several people along my path at various times before this conference, to cause that residue to be spotlighted. You see, God will bring things to our attention, at the appointed time, when we are able to handle it because he wants us healed. Though it caught me off guard, it was right on time for God because not only did I finally need to be free and healed of this, someone else needed to experience this freedom I too was about to receive. So you see, when God exposes things in our lives, it's not to embarrass us. He wants us healed because he has a greater plan for our lives.

One of the ministers from my church spoke on a message entitled "It's There". He was talking about the gift inside of us that's hidden up under all that dirt. He gave a scenario about dirt and how we were created from dirt but one thing he said that really caught my attention was how dirt can weigh us down. It can be a challenge and it is with us daily, dirt that is but then he said we must get past all the dirt to get to the gift that's inside of us because we can't see it past all that dirt, and the world needs that gift within us. The example he used was a gift box buried up under all this dirt, but no one knew it was there. All we could see was the dirt.

The gift under the dirt

Sometimes the people on the outside can only see dirt, your past, things you are struggling with or have struggled with, but God knows what he has placed inside of you. I'm reminded of a story in I Samuel when God told Samuel to choose the next king. The Lord said to Samuel, do not look at his appearance or his physical stature, because I have refused him. For the Lord does not see as man sees; for man looks at the outward appearance, but the Lord looks at the heart." *I Samuel 16:7 (NJKV)* Samuel was impressed with the outer appearance of David's brothers, but they were not the ones God had chosen. I guess David didn't look or appear to be the one whom Samuel thought fit the picture of who God had chosen. Do you fit the picture, or do you feel like you don't have what it takes to fulfill what God has created you to do? God created us all differently and we can't fulfill what he's created us to do if we don't embrace the uniqueness that he's placed down on the inside of us. His plan wasn't for us to compare ourselves with one another, but to be different.

Sometimes we can get focused on the wrong thing and miss out on what God is trying to show us.

We must be reminded that the world is waiting for us, for what's in us to be revealed. There is a gift in you that's waiting to be exposed. When we get past all those things that have been holding us back, we find the gift. There's something there that can be used but no one on the outside can see the gift, all they see is dirt.

Somebody needs to know that they can make it through what you've already experienced. At times we feel like we are the only ones going through what we are experiencing, but we must remember that we are not alone. Someone else may have also experienced something remarkably similar to what you are currently going through.

When we accept Jesus Christ as our Lord and Savior, he allows things in our lives that are not like him to be exposed so that we can be healed. He is "light" and those things that are in the dark areas of our lives, are now being illuminated by the light and can no longer be hidden. You see, he's a loving God.

It's Time to Take the Mask Off

Merriam Webster defines a mask as "a cover or partial cover for the face used for disguise." What does a mask do? Well, for one thing, it hides part of our faces as we now have experienced during this season of the pandemic that we are in. Sometimes we can recognize a person and sometimes we can't. It can even be used to cover up some imperfections a person may have, just like with makeup. But the mask doesn't reveal the whole you, a mask is temporary and can be easily removed if needed.

Well, this mask I'm talking about is invisible. You see, we look good on the outside, but no one really knows or understands what's happening on the inside of us, but God does.

He knows every hurt, pain, and disappointment that we have ever experienced, yet he still loves us, and he wants us healed. With this mask, we have a habit of always saying, I'm good, I'm ok or I'm blessed, when people ask how we are doing. We want the appearance to be that everything is ok. We don't want people who look at us as strong to think that we are weak, especially if we are in a high position or have this great title to our name. We don't want them to know that we're going through anything, forgetting that we are still human and encounter life just like everyone else.

But we must be true to who we are, we must be realistic about our situation. We don't live in fairytale land, though some may want to. The reality is that some of us have experienced some traumatic things in our lives. The Truth is, it's time to finally be rid of that issue and finally be healed. We must take the masks off so the real us can come out of hiding and shine forth and make an impact in the world.

3

CONFRONTATION TIME

Michael Jackson, wrote a song entitled "Man in the Mirror", and part of the lyrics say, "I'm starting with the Man in the Mirror, I'm asking him to change his ways, and no message could have been any clearer if you want to make the world a better place, take a look at yourself, and then make a change". I like those lyrics because they have a powerful meaning that can apply to different things.

Sometimes we must see the ugly truths about ourselves, and it doesn't always look good. That's what confrontation does, and it can be such a hard, uncomfortable, or even difficult thing. People just don't like confrontation or to confront things, especially when it comes to self! I remember when I was younger, I would just say things to people and didn't care how it sounded. Then one day my mom said to me, "It's not what you say, but how you say it, people can't receive it that way". I didn't care how I would say things to people, I just wanted them to know how I felt about the situation. But when it was brought to my attention, it wasn't an easy thing to hear. It's never easy to hear something about yourself, especially when confronted with it by those close to you. But even at the point of confrontation, you can choose to change and do something about it, or just remain the same. *We ALL have a choice*.

Those choices we make or don't make can be a setback for some or a major breakthrough in another's life. When I think about confrontation, I'm not talking about getting in someone's face and giving them a piece of your mind, lol, though at times we want to. I'm talking about dealing with an issue or problem in our life that has caused a negative impact, but for some reason, we just brushed it under the rug or put it in the back of our minds so that we would forget.

Confrontation can be a huge thing to some because people generally just don't like confronting things. It can be negative to some or positive to others. It's all about how you look at it and the impact that it had on your life. My pastor, Bishop Eugene Reeves mentioned in a message he preached years ago – those things that we never confront, they don't go away. So, at some point in our lives, we have to confront things and it might not be easy at times; but if we truly want to get past some of those hurdles and obstacles in our lives that have held us back, we must confront them.

Confronting something from your past can be very painful and it can open a whole "can of worms" as some say, to things that a person once forgot. It causes you to go deep down to deal with an issue. Even some counselors or therapists, take you back to your past or childhood to try to determine the root issue or the source of the problem. So, what does it mean to confront something? It means meet (someone) face to face with hostile or argumentative intent, to challenge, square up to, oppose, resist, or approach. There are so many meanings of this, but it means you must do something about this thing and deal with it once and for all.

One thing that is so important to remember is that God loves us and wants us to be healed and whole. **3 John 1:3 (KJV)** says - "Beloved, I wish above things that thou mayest prosper and be in health, even as thy soul prospereth".

Another important key to remember in confrontation is *acknowledgment.*

There is a story in the bible in *Luke 15:11-32 (KJV)*, which talks about this young man, the prodigal son. He wanted his portion of his inheritance from his father before it was time, and his father decided to give it to him. Well, to make a long story short, he didn't do the right thing with his inheritance and wasted it all. He had to go through a process of living in a tough situation, before realizing all he left behind. He had to arrive at a place of coming to himself (acknowledgment), that what he had done was wrong and that he needed to go back home and make things right with his father, but it was only when he came to himself.

When we *acknowledge*, according to *Oxford Dictionary*, we accept or admit the existence or truth of something. Our eyes are opened to the fact that there is an issue or a problem, and something needs to change. When we come to this place in our lives, then that too is the beginning of our healing process.

Now it's time to release

What does it mean to **release**? Oxford Dictionary defines release as: allow or enable to escape from confinement; set free; allow (something) to move, act, or flow freely.

Releasing something that's been a burden in your heart or your mind for so long can feel like a weight has been lifted. One way to release something is by simply having a conversation with someone.

I briefly shared my story about how I was asked to speak at a conference about *How to Forgive When You Can't Forget* and before I knew it, God has changed part of my message when he spotlighted the residue from the past that I had been carrying from the rape for over twenty years. Though I had ignored it or forgotten about what happened to me years ago, it was time to confront it and God knew exactly the time and place for it to finally happen.

You see, God will keep bringing things to our attention because he loves us and doesn't want things to hold us back or keep us from doing all he created us to do. He also knows when we are ready for what he's about to do in our lives and who will be around to hear our story so they too can come out of what they are in.

That day at the conference, I finally acknowledged and realized that God had been trying to get my attention at so many different times, but I ignored him and the signs as if it didn't apply to me. This taught me that we have the responsibility as well in confrontation, to either respond to God or not if we genuinely want to be healed and free from life's experiences that affected us and left those remnants of *"residue"*.

4

NO SHAME IN HEALING

What is shame you ask? Well, shame is a painful feeling of humiliation or distress caused by the consciousness of wrong or foolish behavior (dictionary – Oxford Languages). So, in our mindset, we think, I don't want anyone else to know. This is what "shame" does. Shame makes you feel like you can't tell anyone or talk to anyone about what happened. You feel as though they will judge you or make you feel worst about the situation, so you shut down again because you can't trust anyone with your heart. How do you tell someone your deep dark secrets anyway? Will they look at you funny or make you feel weird about yourself, or what? This is how I felt, so I erased what happened to me from my mind somehow. Why? Because the reality was that no matter how drunk I was, they had no right to do what they did but how could I justify it, so, I thought.

These thoughts are things that you must fight in your mind, because of what shame does and how it makes you feel. Sometimes we assume how a person is going to react when we share things with them and that's not always good either. The best way with overcoming that part, the fear of another's response, is to find the person you feel most comfortable with and share.

I believe God places the right people in our lives at the right time. There have been times at work, whether I was at my desk, getting coffee in the kitchen, or just walking around the firm, that I would encounter a co-worker. A general conversation would come up and before I knew it, I ended up finding out more about that person or something they were dealing with that I would have never known, in just a few minutes. Afterwards, when I looked back, I thought wow, what just happened. I realized that it was all God's timing, and that they'll always be an opportunity to share our stories with someone. It's just a matter of timing and if we are willing to open up and not allow shame or fear to hold us back.

You see, you want it out of you, that thing that you have been secretly carrying for so long. You don't want this thing, the shame of it, or things that's been having such a hold or control over you to have anymore power.

Some of us have heard the slogan or people say, "I'll take it to my grave". That doesn't make sense at all!! Why would a person carry something that long while they are living, when they can be healed and free from it while here on earth? But again, that's what shame does. It wants to keep that thing secret or hidden but God sent his son Jesus Christ to die on the cross and rise again so that we don't have to carry these hurts, pains, or burdens with us to the grave. *John 10:10 (KJV) says: "The thief cometh not, but for to steal, and to kill, and to destroy; I am come that they may have life and that they might have it more abundantly"*.

God wants us to enjoy life to the fullest and be healed right here on earth and enjoy the life that he has blessed us with.

Can I talk about Peace, true peace? The feeling of relief when you finally release those things that have been hidden and bottled up in you for so long. You feel so much lighter if that's a word, lol.

That's how I felt when I finally shared my story at the conference. It felt like a layer had come off me after twenty years. Imagine that! Carrying something or having something on you for that long and you don't even realize it. Once it was lifted off, it no longer had any control over my mind, thoughts, behaviors, or decisions. You see sometimes things happen to us and we don't realize how it affects us. All we know is that something is left behind like an old scar called *RESIDUE,* that never healed because it was left alone hiding. That's where God's love, grace, and mercy came into place. He loves us so much; he wants us healed. He doesn't want us to carry all of this unnecessary baggage around weighing us down. He wants to take it from us and take it once and for all.

My pastor, Bishop Eugene Reeves wrote the book *"Lord Deliver Me from People".* That book was such an eye-opener for me because we worry so much about what others think about us to the point that it consumes us, and we end up not doing this or that because of "people". We allow people to stop us in our tracks because of their own personal opinions of what they feel we can or cannot do or should or should not do. It's sad but many people look for affirmation from others. Affirmation is good because it can help build us up, but it should not be the only determining factor of what causes us to do a thing or try something new.

So, my question is, do you want to be healed? You might say, that's a silly question, of course I do. But remember, healing has a process and you must be willing to go through the process so you can receive your healing. And it might be a little hard, but you will make it through!

I'm reminded of this story in the bible, in the book of John, Chapter 5 concerning this man who was lame for thirty-eight years!! There was this place called the Pool of Bethesda and every year an angel would come by and stir the water **(John 5:4 KJV)** and anyone could go step in and get healed. The man had an excuse for not being healed. He said every time the angel stirred the waters someone else got ahead of me. Jesus asked him did he want to be healed. You see, when a person has been in a situation for so long, they become content with the issues to a point where that issue is just a part of their norm. They've given up hope of ever overcoming the issue since it's been so long or feel as if nothing good could ever happen to them.

Our mindset must change! Don't copy the behavior and customs of this world, but let God transform you into a new person by changing the way you think **(Romans 12:2 NLT)**. When our minds are changed to see and think in a way that God desires, then we can begin to see and even speak differently. How do we know what we can or can't accomplish if we never try? As the timing approached for the angel to come to stir the water so that this man could be healed, he could have pushed himself, crawled, or did whatever he could do to make it closer so that when the time came, he wouldn't miss his turn. Are you determined? How bad do you want to be healed? Haven't you held on to your pain too long? Are you tired of that pain from the past tormenting you? Are you tired of someone telling you that you are too sensitive, or so easily offended? Don't you want to have a peaceful sleep at night? These are questions only something we can answer ourselves, aside from fear, shame, and even our own bad thinking. We must be so determined when it comes to ourselves that we can't allow anything or anyone to stop us from receiving what we need. Sometimes we must press past our obstacles. At times those obstacles are just negative thoughts in our minds, trying to stop us and make us give up and quit.

There's another story that I love about this woman who had an issue with Blood in the bible. *Luke 8:43-48 (KJV)*. You see, her story was another one where she could have allowed her situation, the thoughts of people, or even the laws in the land at that time to stop her from receiving her healing. After waiting twelve long years, something within her caused her to be so determined to receive her healing that she pressed her way to get what she needed. Despite the fear of what could happen, others looking at her, talking about her, and even judging her because she was really considered to be unclean and shouldn't have even been out in public. So, I'm sure so many other things tried to get in her way to stop her but guess what, she too received her healing because she made up in her mind, no matter what, I'm tired of being in this situation for so long. She had done all that she knew how to do on her own and she was desperate. She found her way to Jesus, her only hope, whom she only *"heard"* was passing through. So, you see, everyone has a story, a history, and a past. But we have to be the one who does something about it and still live to talk about it. Somebody needs to hear our story! Yes, some things have been hard for us, and we can't believe that we experienced the things we went through, but guess what, you're still here. Don't be the one to take it to the grave but choose to be healed now. Life waits for you and that gift inside of you is screaming to finally come out so that you too can help someone's life change!

5

TRANSFORMATION,
IT'S A PROCESS

I was asked to be one of the speakers at this conference entitled "Rags to Riches" and we were given the freedom to come up with our own topic that tied in with the title and the scripture (*2 Corinthians 5:17 NLT*) of the conference. So, I thought about it and prayed about it and just kept thinking, *Rags to Riches?* Wow! For someone to come from *Rags to Riches* is a huge transformation! So, there it was, my topic, just like that! It was so clear because it seemed impossible really, if you think of someone starting at *Rags* then going to *Riches*. They'd have to win the lottery or something major must happen to them, right? This was even greater than that because I thought of it as someone being at a very low place then something miraculous impacts their lives to bring about such a great and major change, a drastic change. This was a *transformation!*

What does it mean to be transformed?

The word "transformation," according to Merriam-Webster, means "a complete or major change in someone or something's appearance, form."

When I think about something that is transformed and turned into something beautiful, I think of the caterpillar. Did you know that they go through a transformation? They go through what is called a metamorphosis to become the beautiful butterfly that they are. What's a metamorphosis you ask? According to Learner's definition, a *metamorphosis* is a dramatic change that some animals and insects go through during their life cycles.

The change is dramatic, and the baby stage looks very different from the adult stage. It's a change of physical form, structure, or substance especially.

So, as you see, transformation is necessary for change, it brings out the beauty and the best within us just like how the butterfly is reflected on the outside. If you think about it, we would never be able to experience and see the beautiful butterflies if they didn't go through the process to be transformed.

"Change is inevitable. Growth is optional" – John Maxwell

Change can be good and uncomfortable at times, but change is necessary. It can bring the best out of you or the worst, but it depends on how we respond to the change or the situation going on. Everything, including seasons, must go through a change or be stuck in the same season all the time. Yes, I know, some of you would love that. Especially to be stuck in Spring or Summer all year long. But we wouldn't have the opportunity to experience anything different. It would be the same thing over and over again. Being opened to change and allowing the transformation process to begin in your life, will allow so many opportunities to be opened for you.

So, what is it that you need to confront today so that your transformation can begin? It's time to dig deep and stop ignoring the signs, red flags, and several confirmations that God has sent through different people to help you.

My transformation

I honestly believe my process began when I finally acknowledged that those stories of women being raped or abused also applied to me. It immediately started when a friend of mine, asked me after a women's conference, in the parking lot, had anything like that ever happened to me. It caused me to think and realize, that yes, that happened to me. And once I came to that place of accepting, yes, the good, bad, and ugly of what had happened, then God began to present opportunities for me to share my story so that the healing process could continue.

As I drew closer to God and my life began to change, those things that were hidden began to come up and God sent people across my path at conferences and many other places to bring things to my attention, but I brushed it off. So, you see, we can ignore the signs, the sleepless nights, the bad repeated habits or behaviors or we can realize that there is so much more to us than where we are at and where we've been. We must allow ourselves to go through this process of change if we want to experience God's best.

Are you ready for a change?

Only you can respond to that question of change. But if you are desperate and want to see things change in your life, you must be willing to acknowledge that the issues you have experienced were real, then confront them and allow the healing to take place so that transformation can also take place in your life.

Final Thought

True healing and peace from anything that we encounter in life, only come from God. We can substitute things like alcohol, drugs, or any type of addictive behavior to temporarily soothe the pain of the past or even our present, but it is only temporary. God wants to heal our brokenness and wants us whole. Remember, no one in the world is perfect and we have all sinned and done things we weren't proud of, but we must forgive others and even ourselves.

If you want that true peace and healing once and for all, and you haven't experienced a personal relationship with the Prince of Peace Jesus Christ, I'd love to lead you into prayer. That is why God sent his only son to die on the cross for our sins because we were lost and needed saving. *John 3:16-17 (NLT)* – "For this is how God loved the world: He gave[a] his one and only Son so that everyone who believes in him will not perish but have eternal life. [17] God sent his Son into the world not to judge the world, but to save the world through him".

Romans 10:9-10 (NLT) – "If you openly declare that Jesus is Lord and believe in your heart that God raised him from the dead, you will be saved. [10] For it is by believing in your heart that you are made right with God, and it is by openly declaring your faith that you are saved".

Things will happen to us in life that will affect us, there's no denying that and we must be realistic about it, but we have to learn the proper way of dealing with it so that it doesn't become *Residue* and remain.

Here is a simple prayer:

Dear Lord Jesus, I want to experience true peace in my life. Today, I make the choice to follow you as my Lord and Savior. I ask that you forgive me of all my sins and heal me of my past, in Jesus' name I pray, Amen!

Printed in the United States
by Baker & Taylor Publisher Services